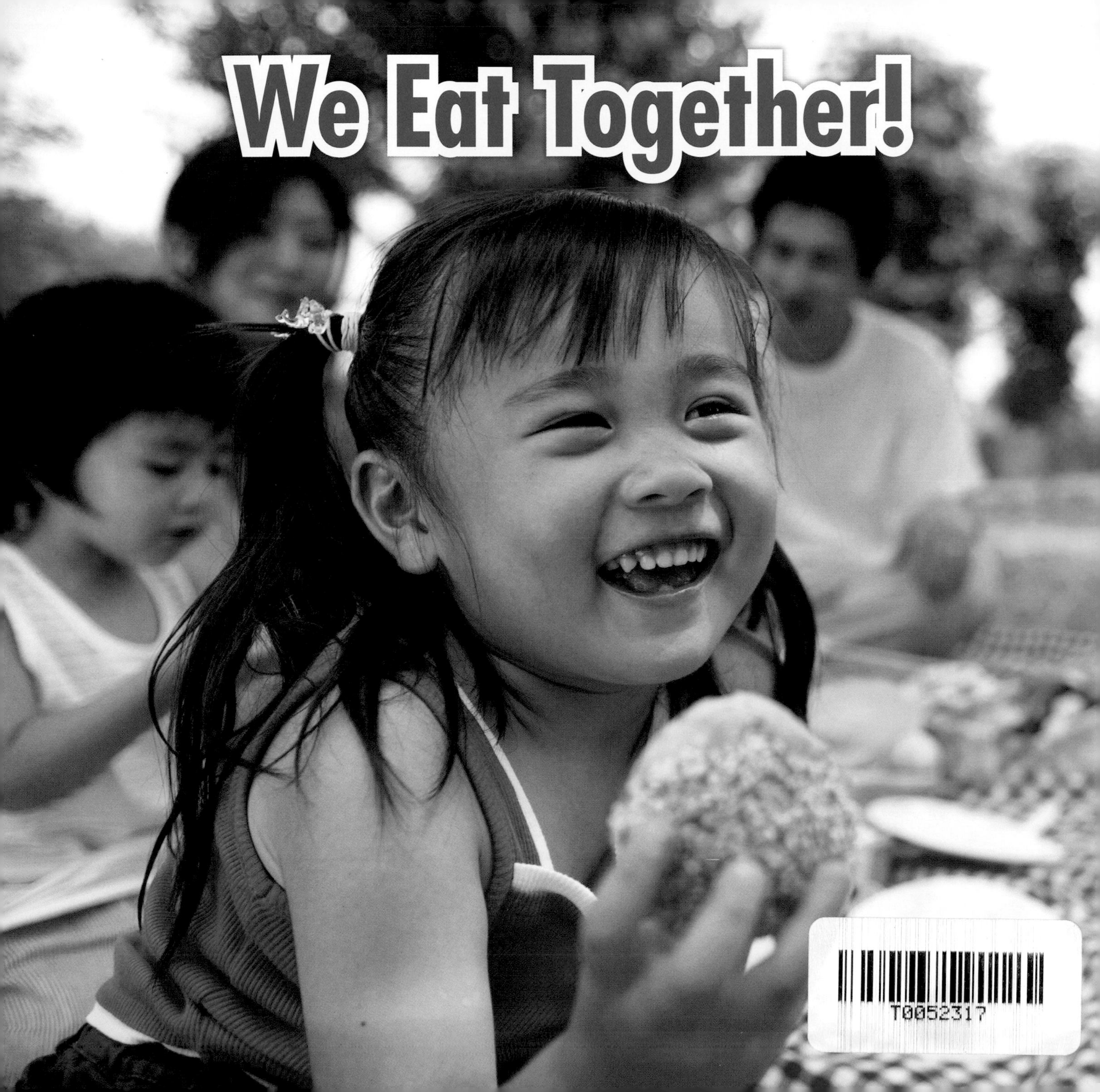
We Eat Together!

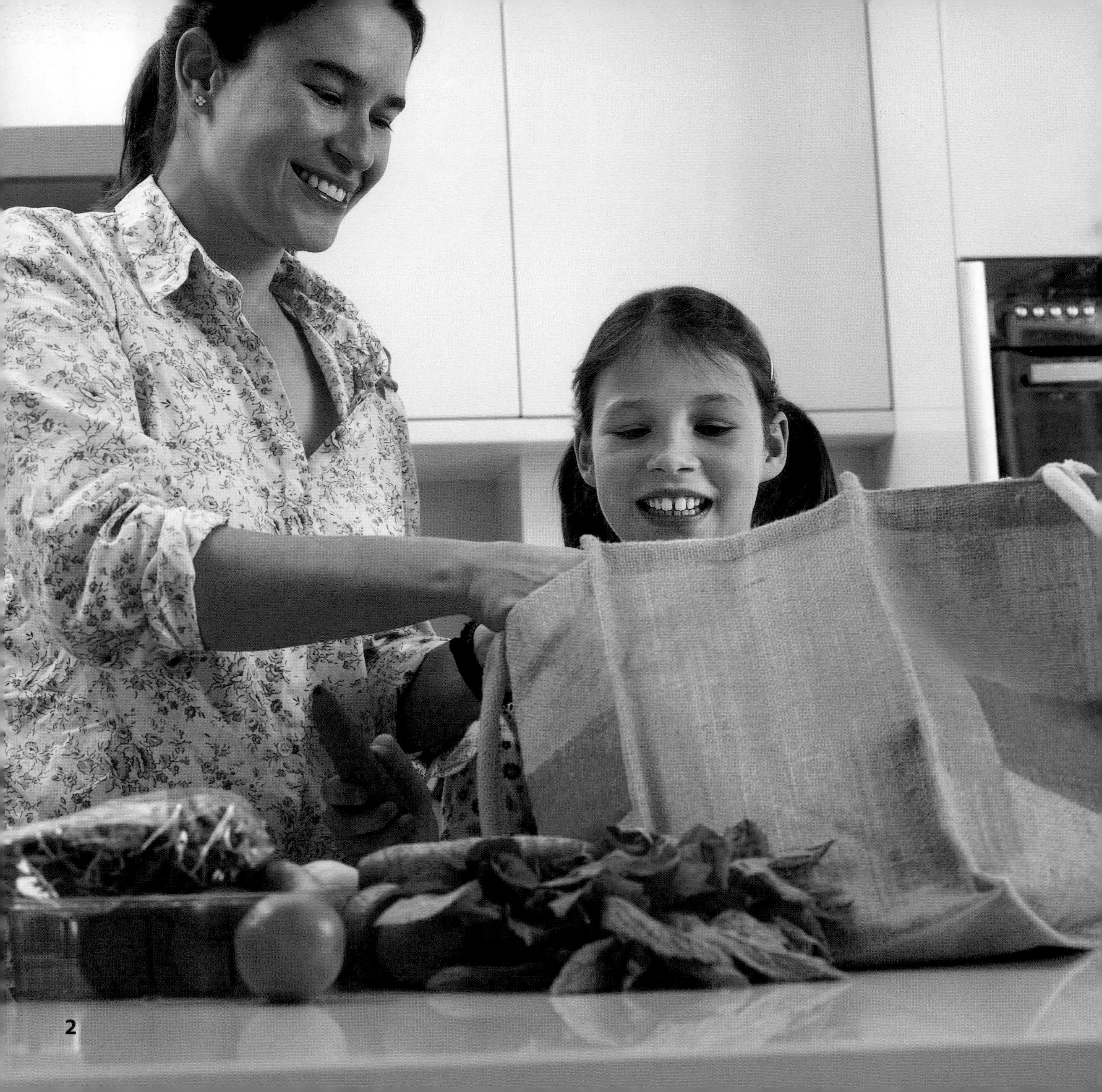

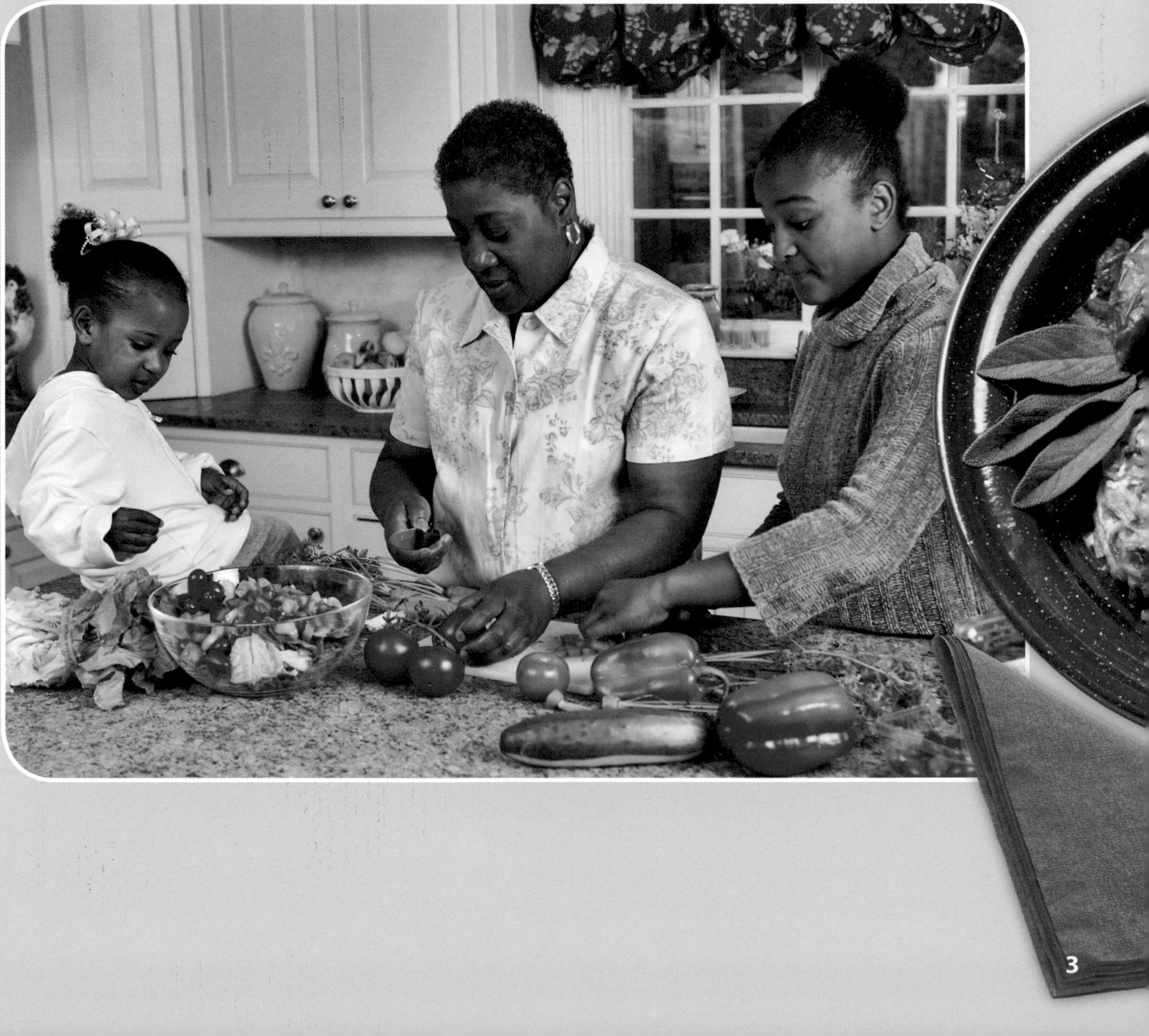

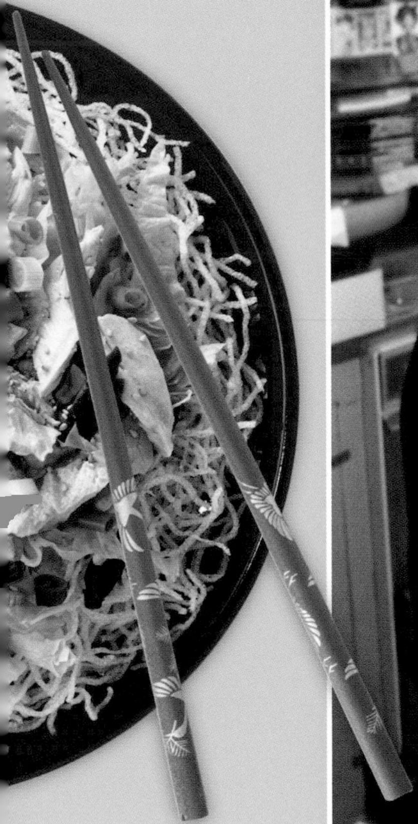

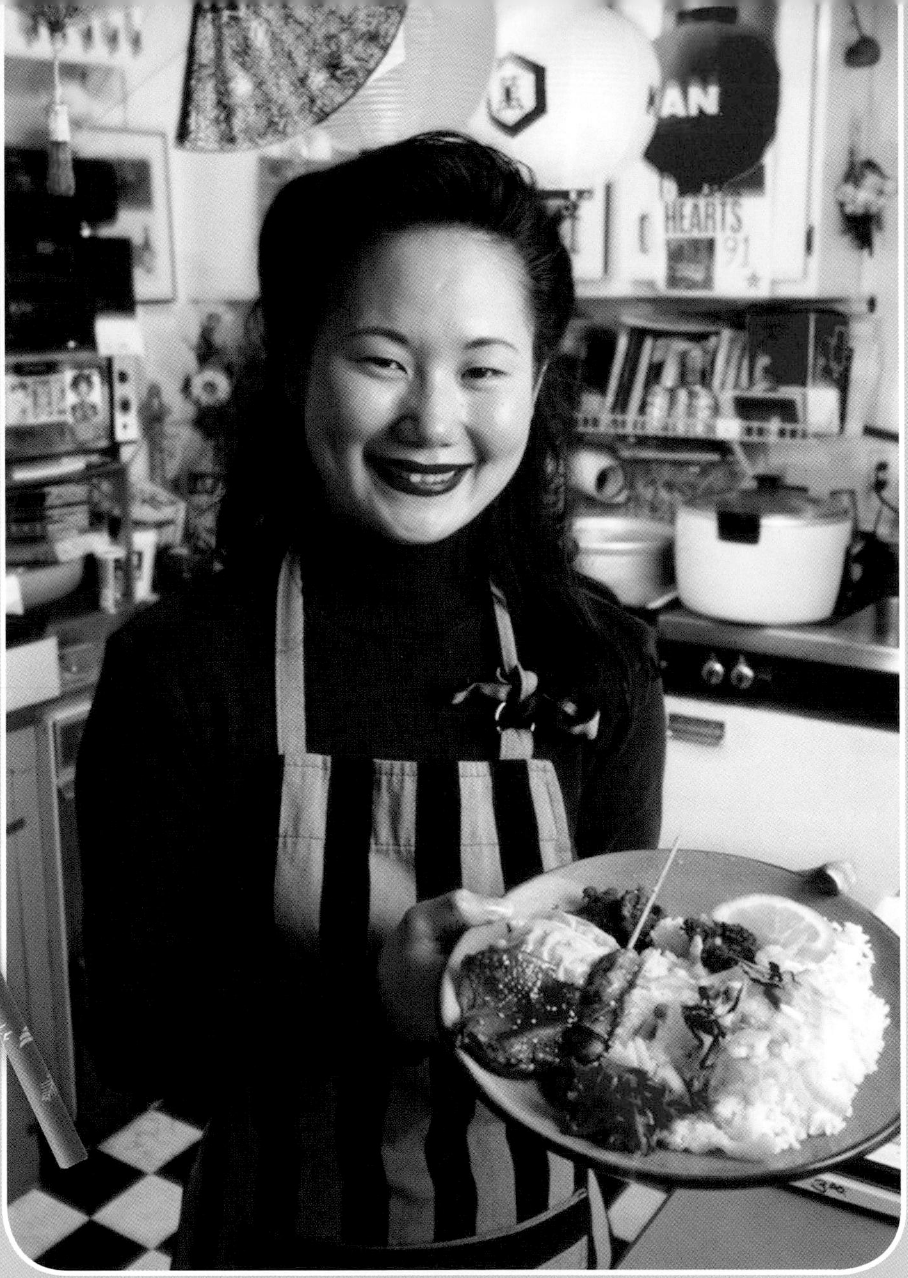
HEARTS
91

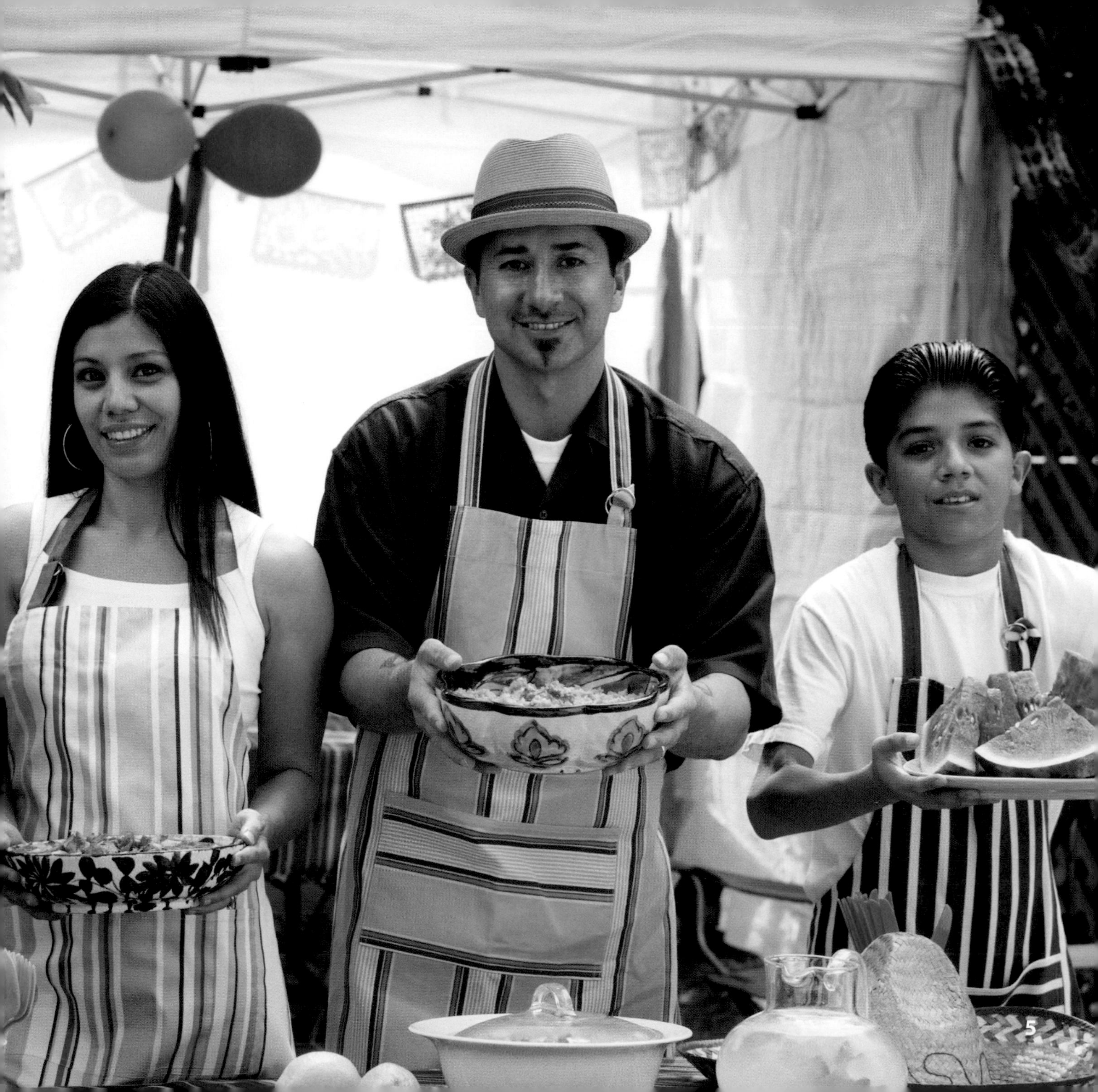

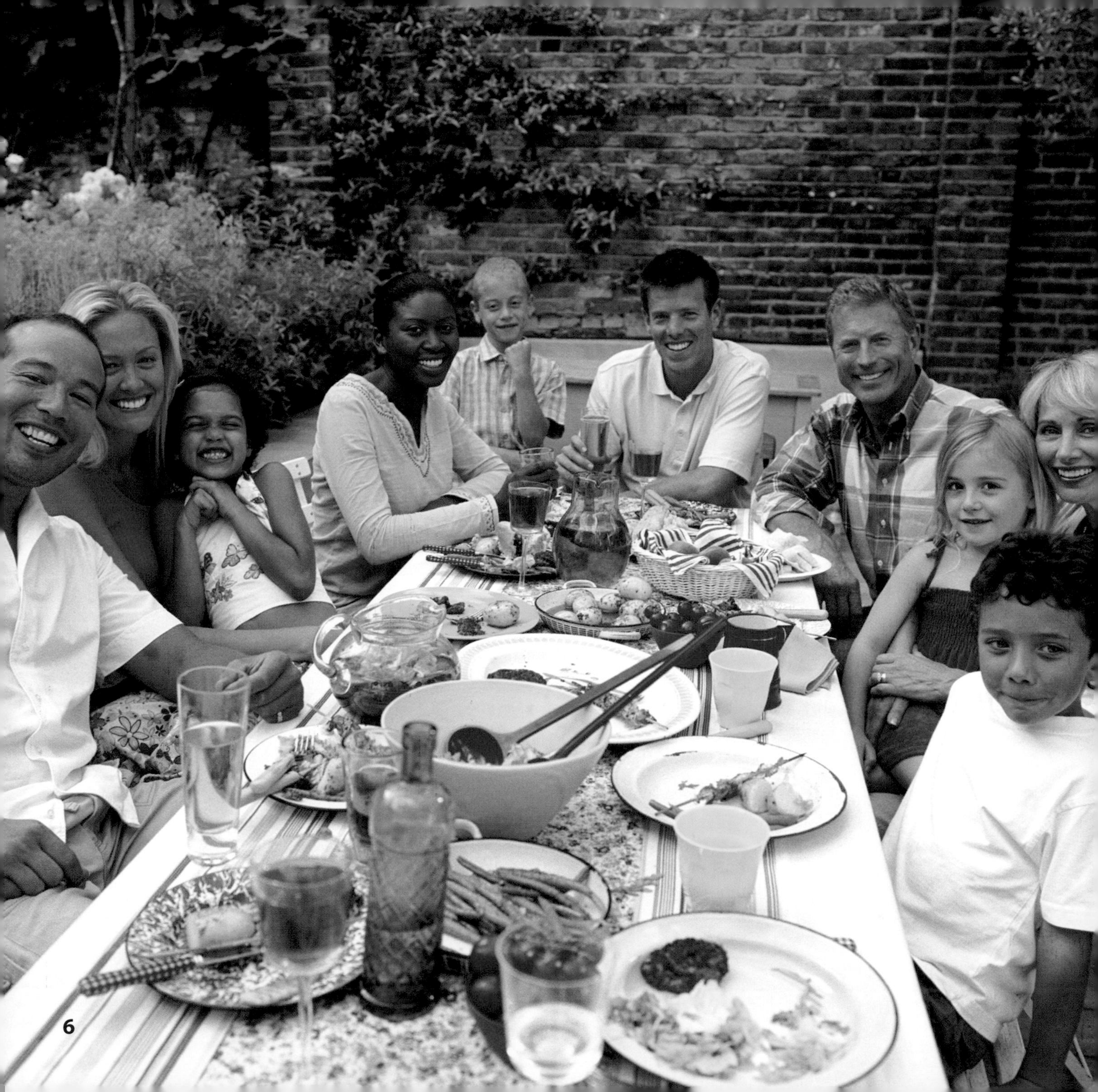

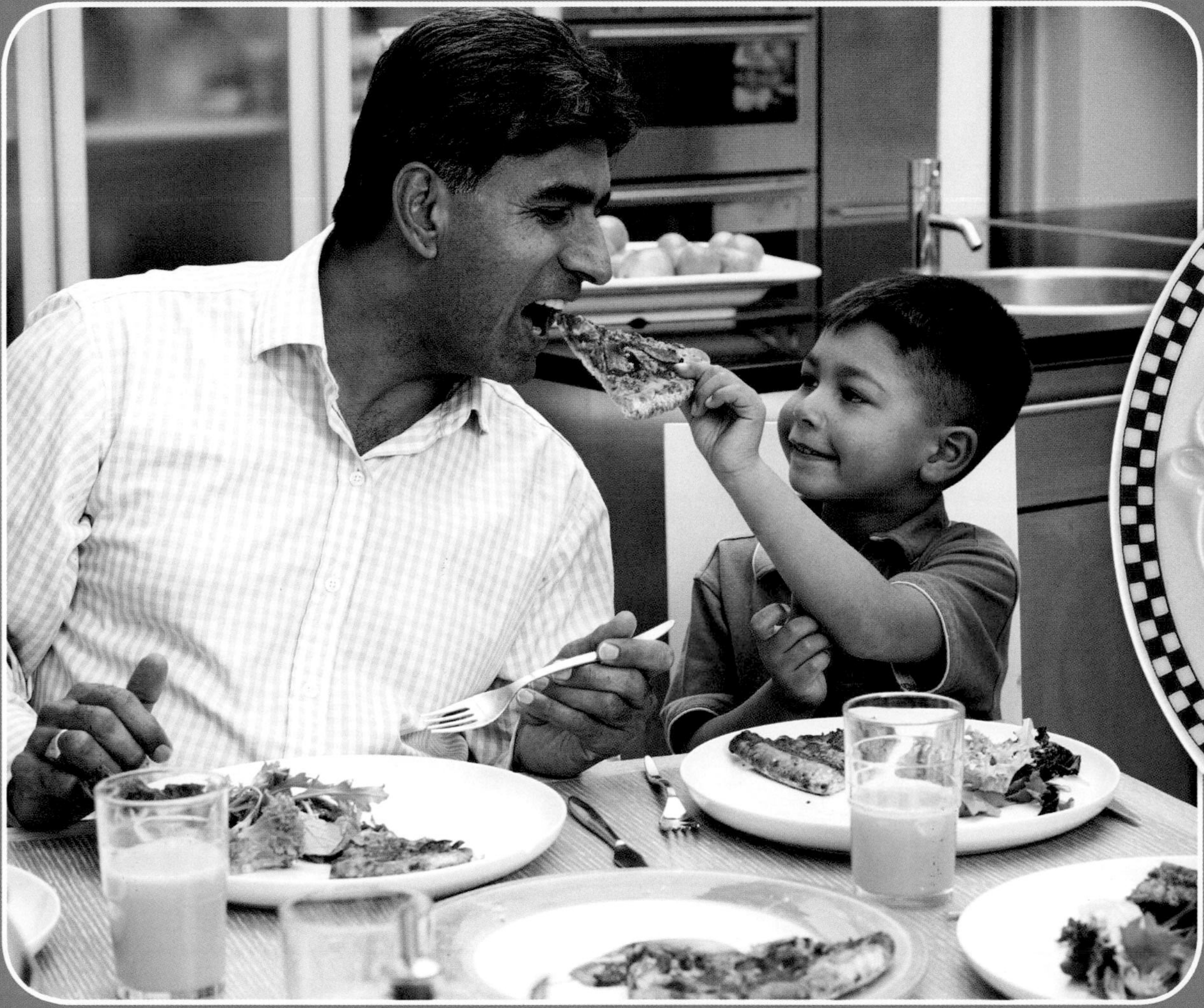

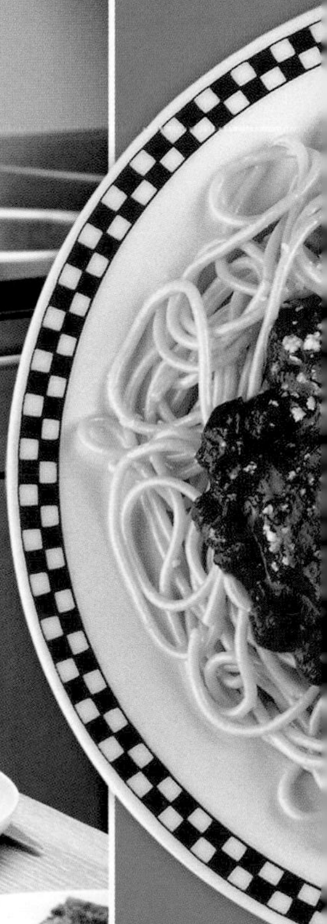

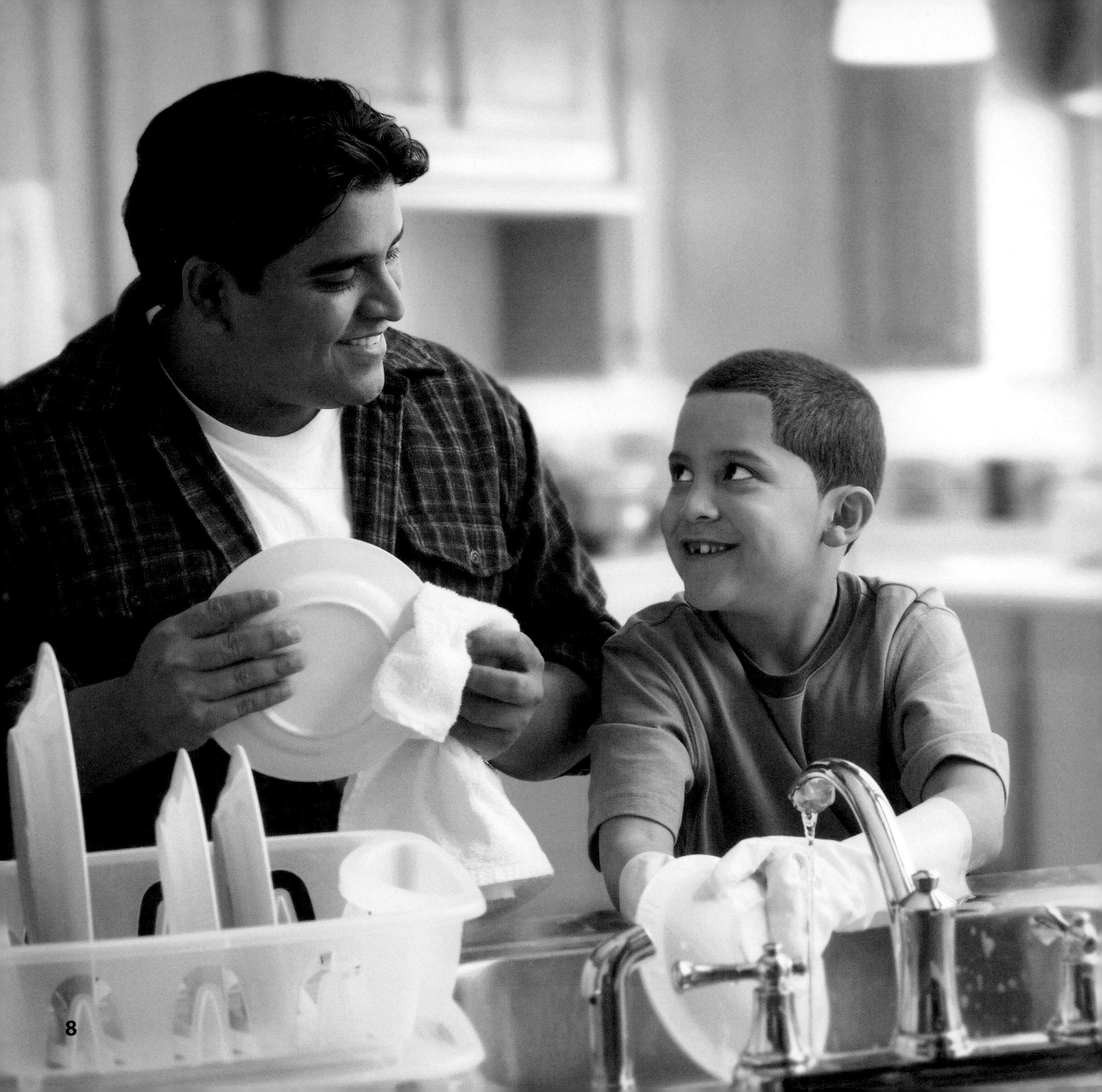